Best Ever
Paper
Planes
that really fly
Paul Jackson

CONTENTS

The World of Paper Planes

Welcome to the exciting world of paper planes! All the planes in this book are superb fliers and can be made from ordinary paper. Some will fly slowly and gracefully, while others will perform exciting acrobatic maneuvers.

The experts achieve perfect results by folding their planes very accurately and throwing them with special techniques. Look for the throwing instructions with each plane so that you can make your planes really fly! If your plane takes a nose-dive, try again, or check that you have folded it exactly as the drawings show.

Why not set up paper planes competitions and games with your friends? Find the plane that flies the longest distance, for the longest time, or can do the best acrobatics. See whose plane performs best! You can even change the designs slightly or design your own planes — see the design tips at the back of this book.

 # Read This!

Here are some important tips to help make your planes fly really well.

- **Press every crease firmly**   Sharp creases help a plane cut through the air smoothly. Use the back of your nail to strengthen the creases.

- **Fold on a table**   Always fold on a hard, flat surface so that you can make firm creases.

- **Follow the steps carefully**   When folding, keep checking to make sure your model looks like the step-by-step drawings. If it doesn't ... don't panic! Just unfold one or two of the new creases until your model looks like an earlier drawing, then try again.

- **Read the "Throwing" instructions**   You may need to use a different throwing technique for each plane. Some need to be thrown hard, others gently. Some are held and thrown in strange ways, so read the tips to get the best results.

- **Find the "point of balance"**   Many planes fly best when held at the "point of balance." To find this point, hold the plane loosely with your thumb and finger, then move your hand toward the nose or toward the tail until the plane doesn't tip over. When the plane stays level in your hand, you have found the point of balance.

- **Safety First**   Never throw a pointed-nosed plane at anyone — the nose can be very sharp and dangerous.

1 If your plane flies quickly upward, stops, and drops like a stone, this is called "stalling." Try curling the back of the wings gently downward. This will make the plane fly level.

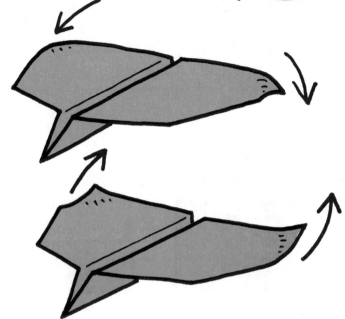

2 If your plane flies quickly downward, this is called "nose-diving." Try curling the back of the wings gently upward. This will make the plane fly level.

3 If your plane still doesn't fly, try adjusting the angle across the wings. This angle is called the "dihedral." Try these dihedral shapes to see which is best for your plane.

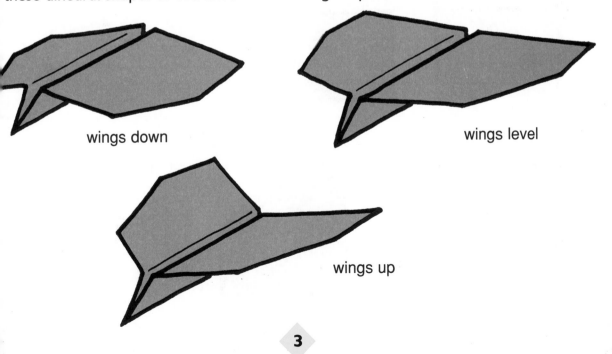

wings down

wings level

wings up

Symbols

These simple symbols explain how the planes are made. You will see them in the step-by-step instructions throughout this book. Make sure you understand the difference between a valley fold and a mountain fold. If you confuse them, your planes will be made inside-out!

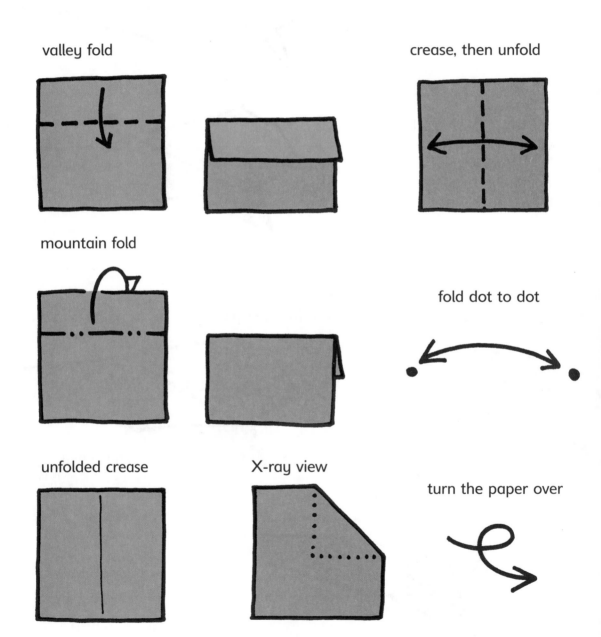

valley fold

crease, then unfold

mountain fold

fold dot to dot

unfolded crease

X-ray view

turn the paper over

Sharpshooter

The very slim nose helps this design cut through the air quickly. Step 1 begins with the paper already folded four ways across the middle.

 Use a square of paper.

1

2

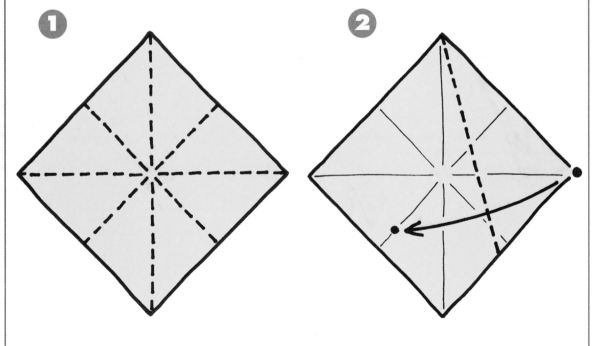

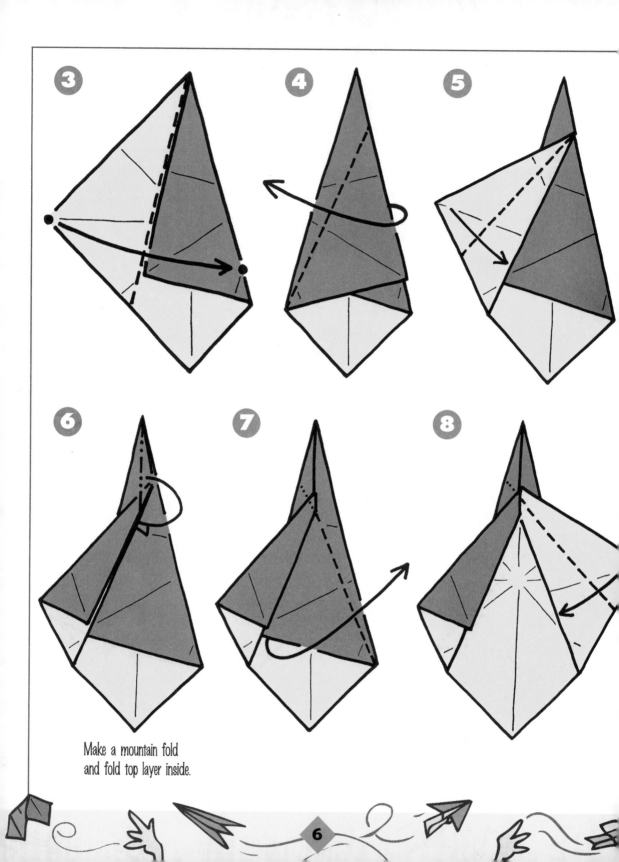

Make a mountain fold
and fold top layer inside.

9

Fold and tuck the tips all the way under.

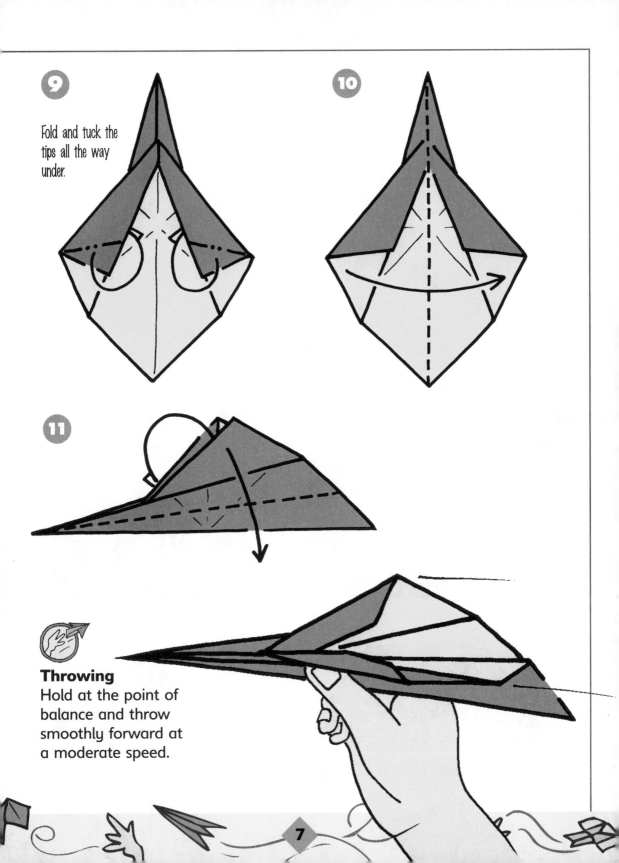

10

11

Throwing
Hold at the point of balance and throw smoothly forward at a moderate speed.

Delta Wing

Triangular planes don't usually fly well, because the shape is too simple. However, this plane flies superbly! The secret here is to fold the wings accurately, in Steps 5 to 7. Start with paper folded in quarters as shown.

 Use European A4 paper or American 8½ x 11-inch paper.

1

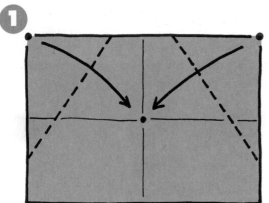

2

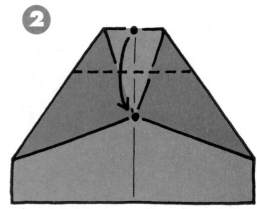

3

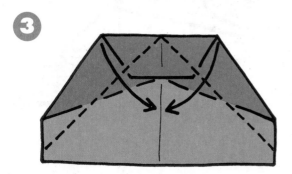

4

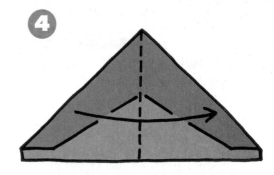

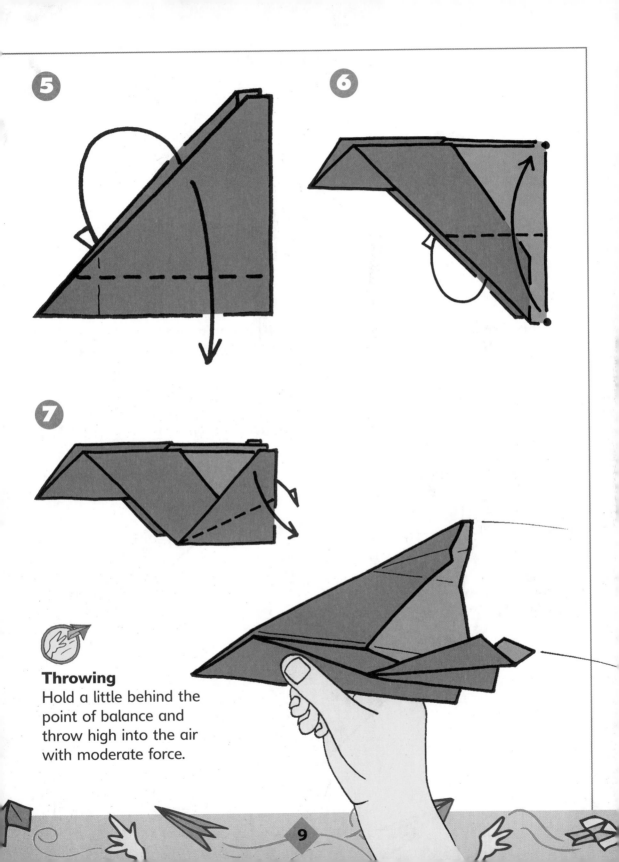

5

6

7

Throwing
Hold a little behind the point of balance and throw high into the air with moderate force.

Hawk

This lively, acrobatic flier is an exciting performer, but be careful to fold it accurately for best results. Experiment with the position of the creases at Step 7. Use a square of paper that has already been creased from corner to corner twice, to make two diagonals.

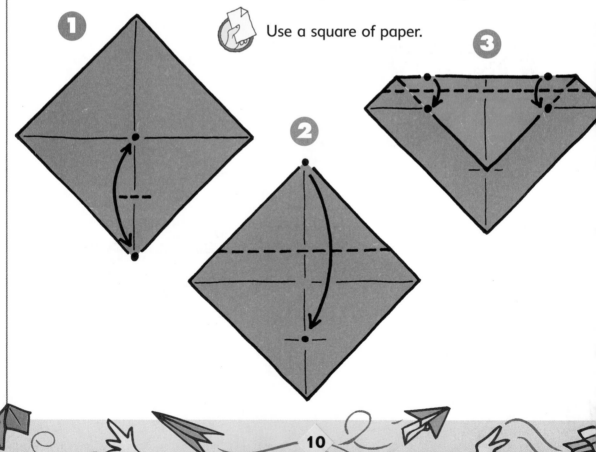

Use a square of paper.

4

5

6

7 Check page 4 for the different folds needed.

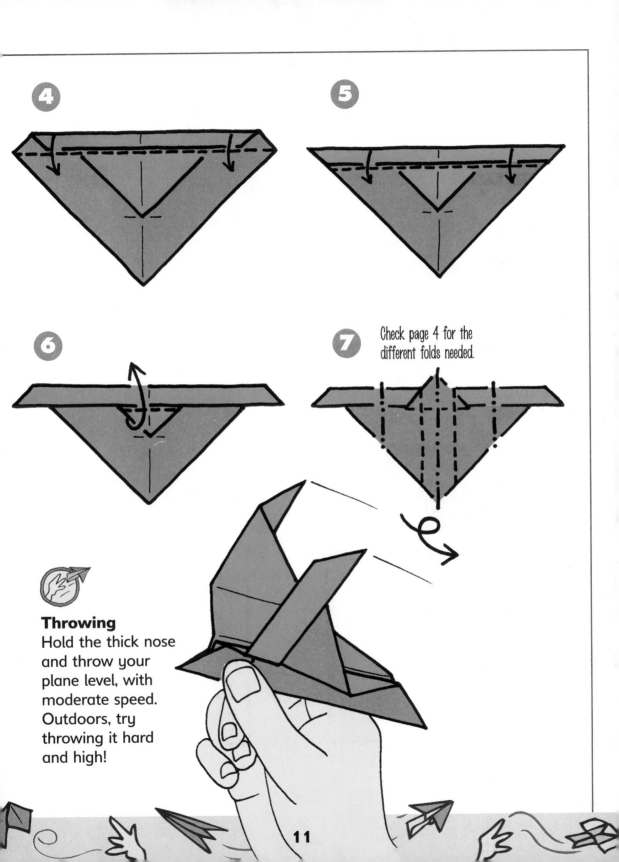

Throwing
Hold the thick nose and throw your plane level, with moderate speed. Outdoors, try throwing it hard and high!

Hoop-nosed Scooter

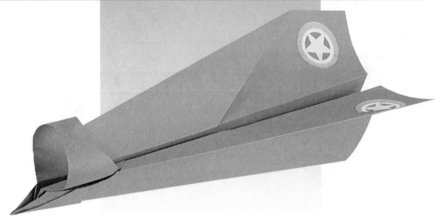

What a peculiar nose! Nevertheless, this strange-looking craft is an excellent flier. Let corners A and B flip into view between steps 2 and 3, and then tuck into each other at the end.

 Use European A4 paper or American 8½ x 11-inch paper.

1
A ... B
C ... D

2 Let the corners flip out as you fold.

B ... A
D C

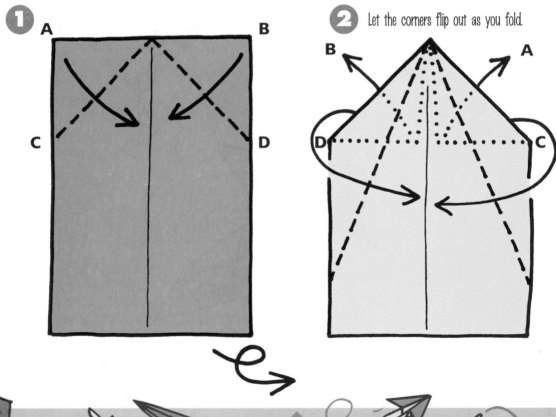

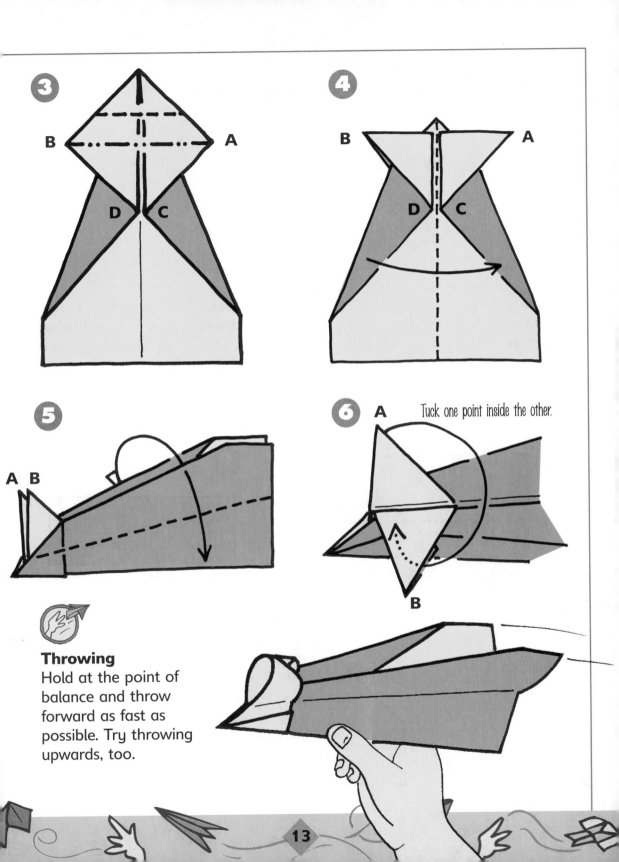

3

B   A

D   C

4

B   A

D   C

5

A B

6   A   Tuck one point inside the other.

B

Throwing

Hold at the point of balance and throw forward as fast as possible. Try throwing upwards, too.

Split Wing

Split wing craft are usually poor fliers, because the missing fuselage makes them unstable. The fuselage is the main body of the plane, between the nose and the tail. However, the small tail-lets seen here help to stabilize this design in flight.

 Use European A4 paper or American 8½ x 11-inch paper, cut in half lengthwise.

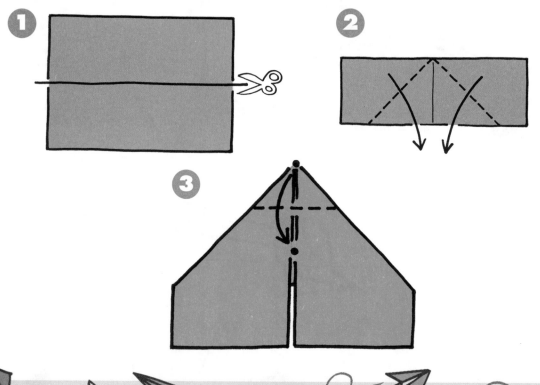

4

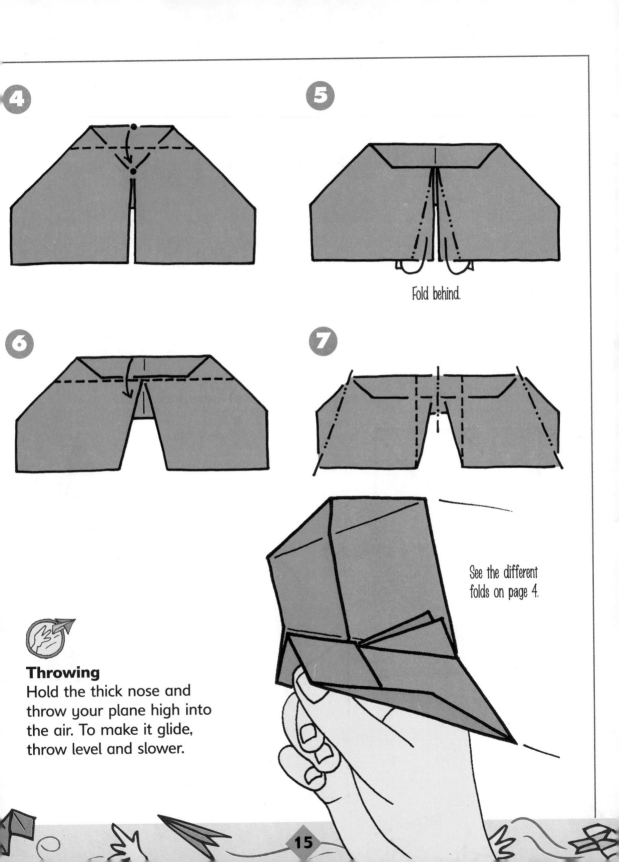

5

Fold behind.

6

7

See the different
folds on page 4.

Throwing

Hold the thick nose and
throw your plane high into
the air. To make it glide,
throw level and slower.

Modified Classic Dart

This elegant flier looks like the well-known Paper Dart at Step 3, but then it's folded differently to create a plane that is shorter and wider than the original dart, and which glides more slowly.

 Use European A4 paper or American 8½ x 11-inch paper.

1

2

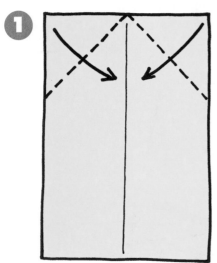

3

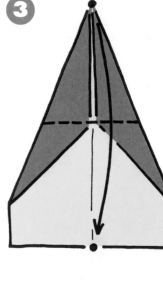

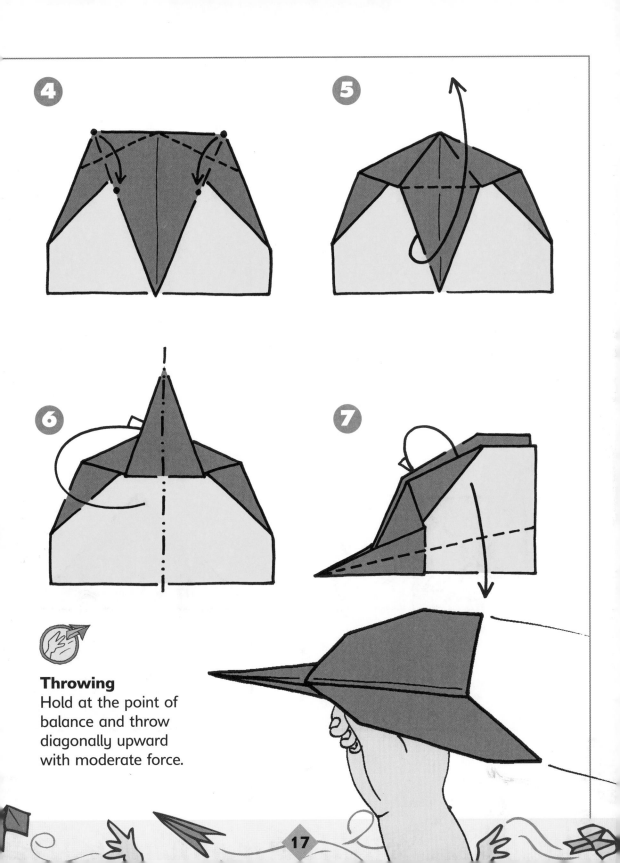

Throwing
Hold at the point of
balance and throw
diagonally upward
with moderate force.

17

Canard

"Canard" wings are the small wings sometimes added to real planes for extra stability and lift. Here, they help an excellent paper plane fly even better. Let corners A and B flip into view between Steps 3 and 4, and see the shape of the paper change dramatically.

Use a square of paper.

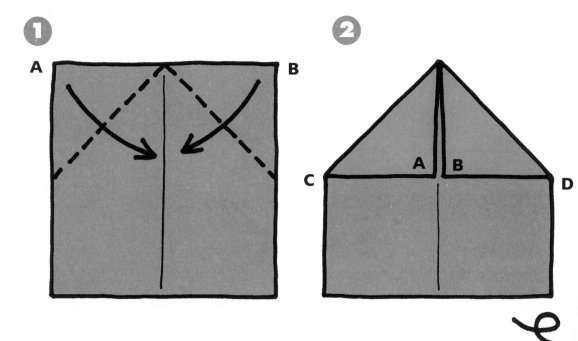

1

A ⟍ ⟋ B

2

A B
C D

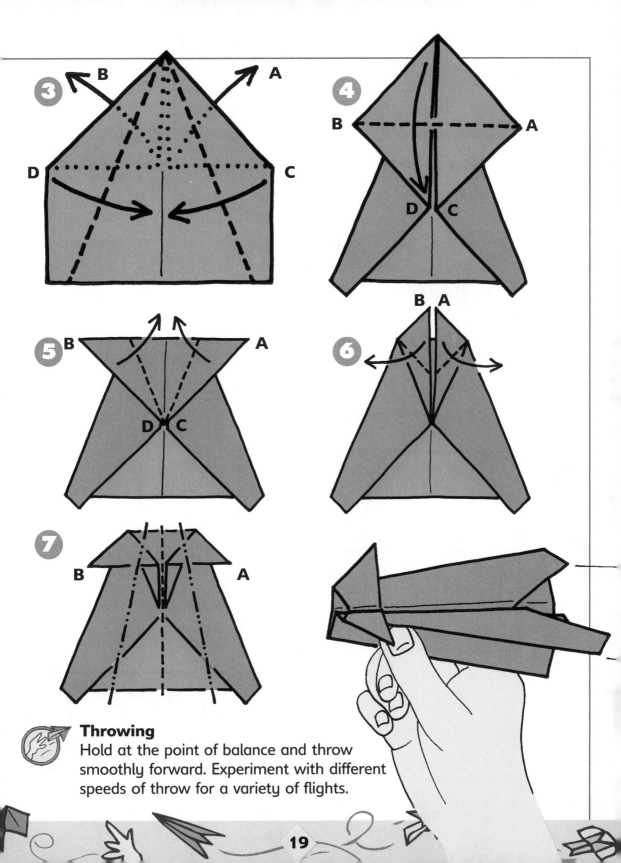

3 B A

D C

4 B A

D C

5 B A

D C

6 B A

7 B A

Throwing
Hold at the point of balance and throw
smoothly forward. Experiment with different
speeds of throw for a variety of flights.

Sleek Streak

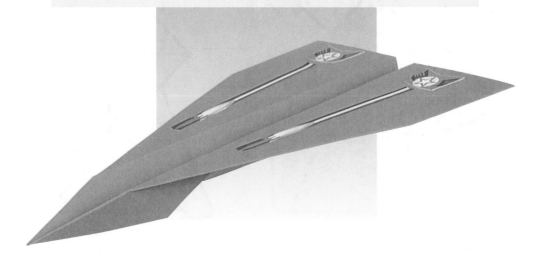

The long, elegant lines of this design make it one of the best-looking of all paper planes ... and it flies brilliantly, too!

 Use European A4 paper or American 8½ x 11-inch paper.

1

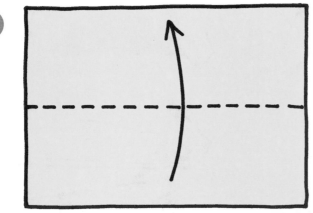

2

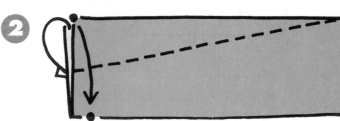

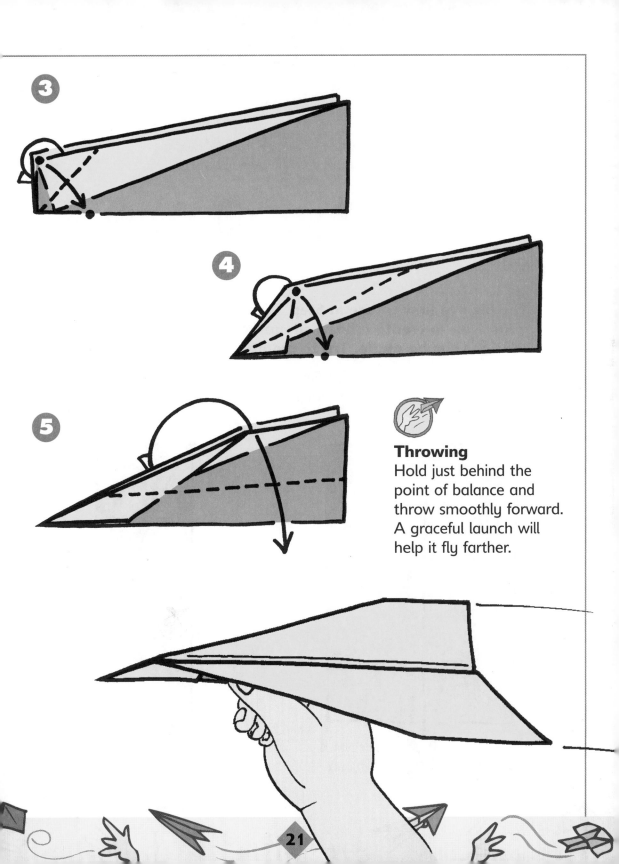

3

4

5

Throwing
Hold just behind the
point of balance and
throw smoothly forward.
A graceful launch will
help it fly farther.

Manta Wing

The bizarre first crease in Step 2 is actually very sensible. It's a good way to create a basic shape from which many interesting designs can be made. Try to create your own original design!

 Use European A4 paper or American 8¹⁄₂ x 11-inch paper.

1

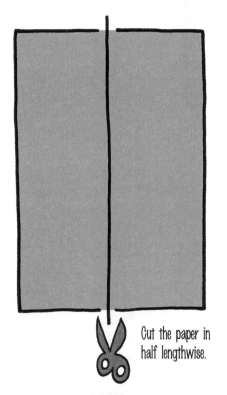

Cut the paper in half lengthwise.

2

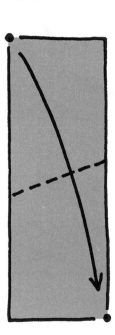

3

4

5

6 See the different folds on page 4.

Throwing

Hold at the point of balance and throw slightly upward with moderate force. To make your Manta fly in loops, hold it right in front of the tail and throw it high.

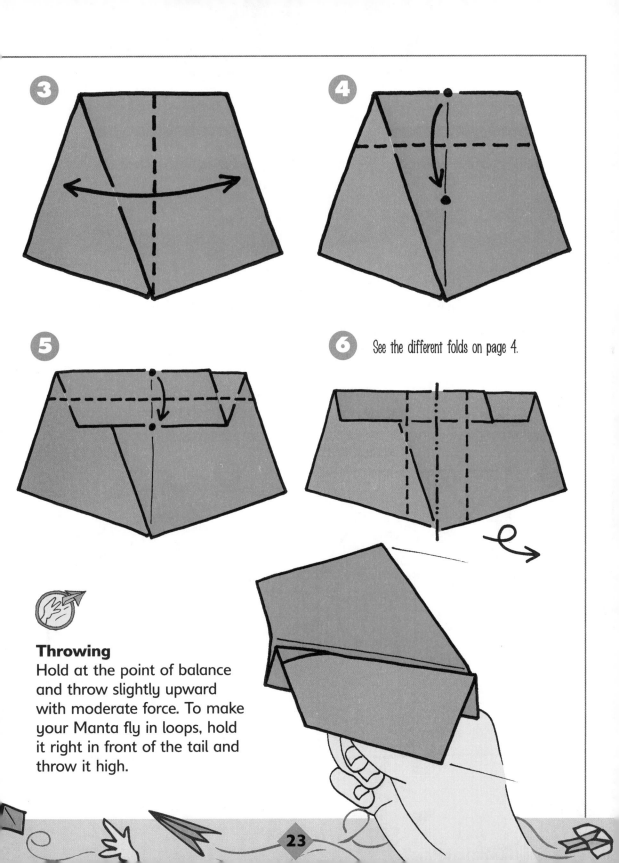

Classroom Cruiser

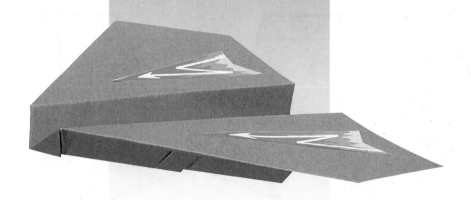

Of all the planes in the book, this is the most stable flier and the easiest to fly. Its balance is perfect, and it will fly a great distance.

 Use European A4 paper or American 8½ x 11-inch paper.

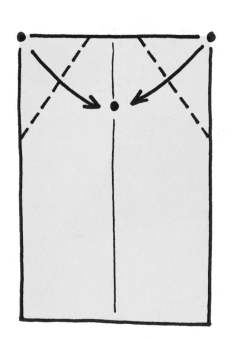

1

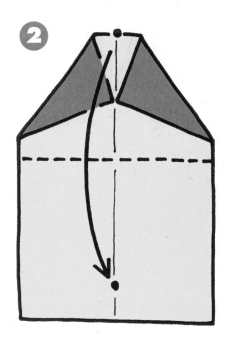

2

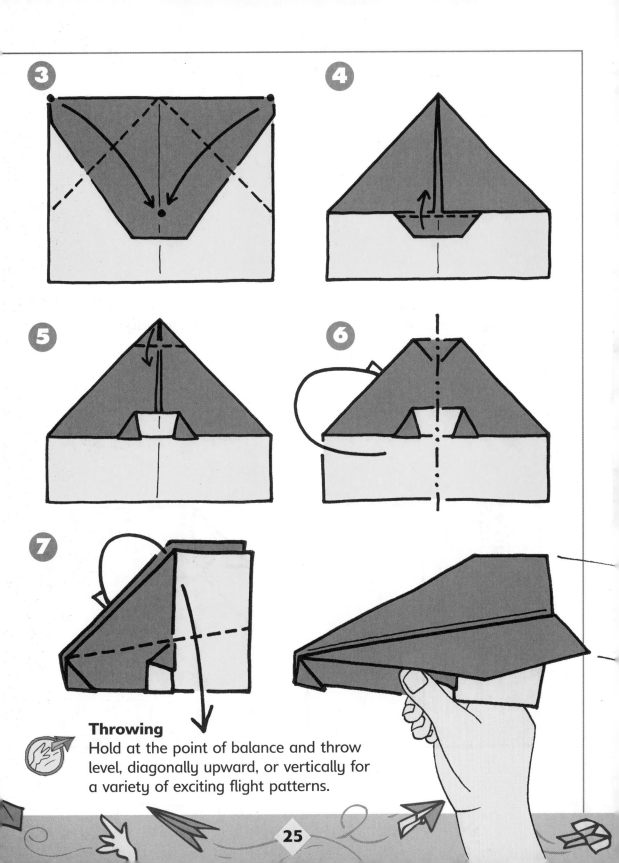

Throwing

Hold at the point of balance and throw level, diagonally upward, or vertically for a variety of exciting flight patterns.

Bottle-nosed Bomber

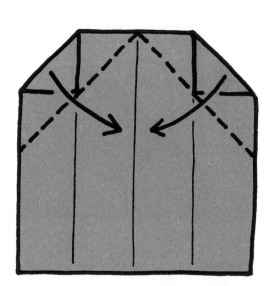

This design has a very unusual nose! It gives this otherwise plain plane a very special shape. Use a square of paper already creased into quarters, as shown.

 Use a square of paper.

1

2

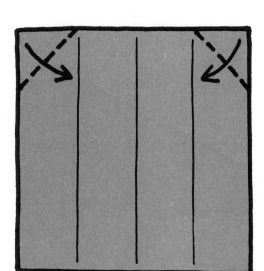

3

4

5

6

7

Throwing

Hold at the point of balance and throw hard and high. You could also try throwing it slightly downward at great speed!

Bullseye Dart

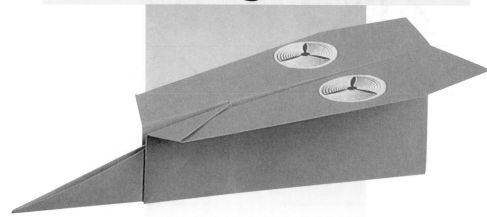

Note how Step 10 locks the nose tightly shut. This lock creates a plane that flies with remarkable accuracy — ideal for target games. Let corners A and B flip into view between Steps 2 and 3. The shape of the paper changes as you fold.

 Use European A4 paper or American 8¹/₂ x 11-inch paper.

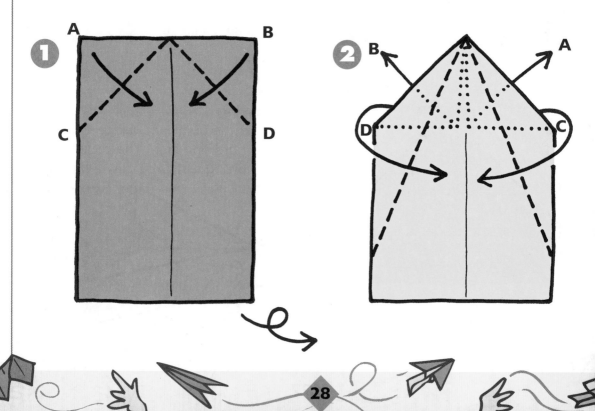

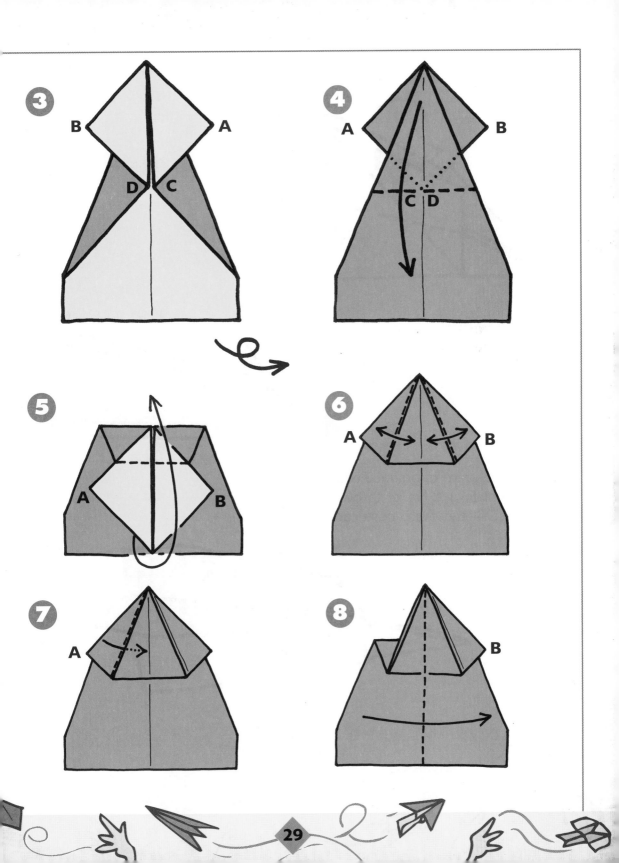

9

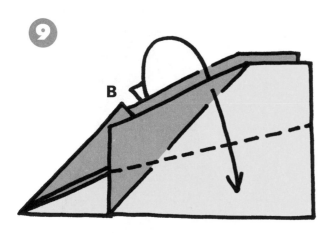

B

10

B   Fold over and tuck in to lock the nose.

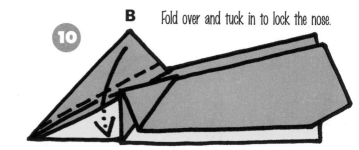

Throwing

Hold at the point of balance and aim carefully at a distant target. Never throw a paper plane at anyone — the sharp nose can be dangerous.

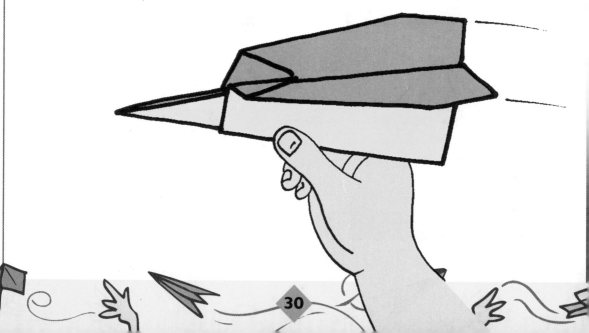

Now Design Your Own Planes!

Designing paper planes is much easier than you think — you just have to follow a few simple rules.

1 Put the Weight at the Front

Whatever shape your plane may be, it must always have a heavy nose. So when folding, find ways to fold in more layers of paper at the front, and ways to keep the layers thin at the tail.

2 Experiment!

You probably won't create the world's greatest paper plane on your very first attempt. To improve it, try adding or reducing weight in the nose, widening or narrowing the wings, adding flaps or fins to the wings, or changing the shape of the paper from a rectangle to a square (or from a square to a rectangle). The more ideas you try, the better your plane will fly. Try throwing it in different ways, too.

3 Fresh Planes Fly Best

A sheet of paper that's been folded and unfolded many times will become criss-crossed with old creases. These old creases stop the air from flowing smoothly over a plane, and it won't fly well. So, to test a design you like, fold it again on a fresh sheet of paper.

4 Read Page 3

A plane may fly better if you bend the rear corners of the wings up or down, or change the dihedral, as explained on page 3. Also, remember to fold accurately and to press the creases down firmly.

Good luck, and have fun!

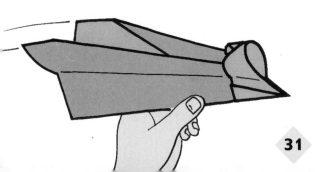

This edition published in 1998 by Flying Frog Publishing,
Auburn, Maine 04210

First published in Great Britain in1998 by
Michael O'Mara Books Limited, 9 Lion Yard,
Tremadoc Road, London SW4 7NQ

Best Ever Paper Planes That Really Fly © 1998 Paul Jackson

Designed by Chris Leishman Design

Printed in Canada